For Michele —J. J.
To Nick, for all his love and support —S.S.B.

This book is available in two editions:
Library binding by Lerner Publications Company
Soft cover by First Avenue Editions
241 First Avenue North
Minneapolis, MN 55401

Library of Congress Cataloging-in-Publication Data

Jansen, John, 1956-
   Class act : riddles for school / by John Jansen ; pictures by
Susan Slattery Burke.
      p.   cm. — (You must be joking!)
   ISBN 0-8225-2345-0 (lib. bdg.) ISBN 0-8225-9673-3 (pbk.)
   1. Riddles, Juvenile. 2. Schools—Juvenile humor. [1. Riddles.
2. Jokes. 3. Schools—Wit and humor.] I. Burke, Susan Slattery,
ill. II. Title. III. Series.
PN6371.5.J35 1995
818'.5402—dc20   94-19554

D1511764

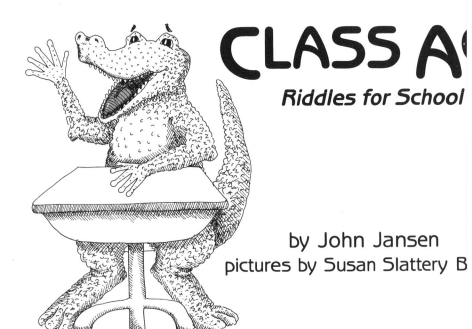

CLASS A

Riddles for School

by John Jansen

pictures by Susan Slattery B

Lerner Publications Company • Minr

Q: Where did the math student eat lunch?

A: At the multiplication table.

Q: Why did the math student bring a ruler to bed?
A: She wanted to see how long she slept.

Q: Why did the girl break her leg before the school play?
A: She wanted to be in the cast.

Q: Why did the student bring his glasses home?
A: To study for the eye test.

Q: Did the teacher write with his left or right hand?
A: Neither. He wrote with a pencil.

Q: What did the science teacher say was at the center of Earth?
A: The letter ''r.''

Q: What did the witch teach in school?

A: Spelling.

Q: Where do baby cows eat their school lunches?

A: In the calf-eteria.

Q: Where do you eat lunch if you have a cold?

A: In the cough-eteria.

Q: Why did the teacher need glasses?
A: She had bad pupils.

Q: Why did the students wear sunglasses?
A: It was an illuminating lesson.

Q: Why did the teacher wear sunglasses?
A: Her students were very bright.

Q: What's the best way to catch a school of fish?
A: With bookworms.

Q: What's the difference between an angler and a bad student?

A: One baits his hooks, the other hates his books.

Q: What color did the art teacher paint the sun and wind?

A: He painted the sun rose and the wind blue.

Q: What's black when it's clean and white when it's dirty?

A: A chalkboard.

Q: What did the teacher say when the student wrote WETHR?

A: "That's the worst spell of weather we've had in a long time."

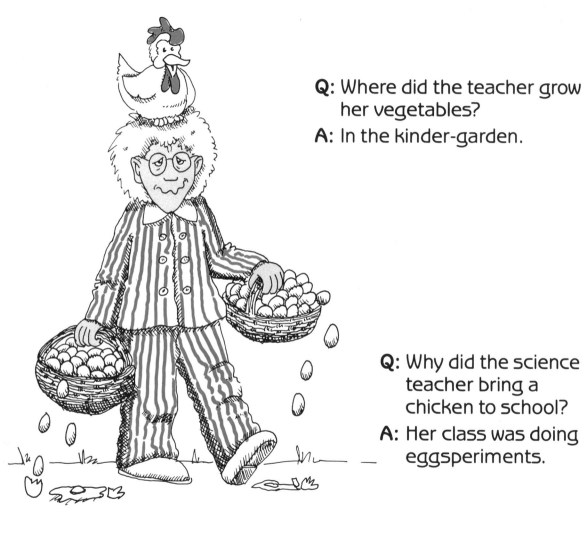

Q: Where did the teacher grow her vegetables?

A: In the kinder-garden.

Q: Why did the science teacher bring a chicken to school?

A: Her class was doing eggsperiments.

Q: Why did the alligator do well in school?

A: He always gave snappy answers.

Q: Was the student in a bad mood during finals?

A: No, she was just a little testy.

Q: Why did the student give his report card a parachute?

A: All his grades were falling.

Q: Why did the naughty student hang around school?

A: Because he was suspended.

Q: How do scholars get across the sea?

A: They use scholarships.

Q: How did the writer get across the water?

A: She took the penmanship.

Q: Why should you work on your penmanship?

A: It's the write thing to do.

Q: Where did the student write his poems?

A: Under the poet-tree.

Q: Why was the geometry
teacher so confusing?

A: Because he talked in circles.

Q: Why did the student hate
learning about Egypt?

A: She was in denial.

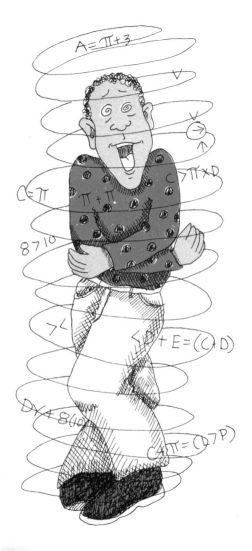

Q: What did the science teacher say when she was asked, "Which is faster, heat or cold?"

A: She said "Heat, because you can catch cold."

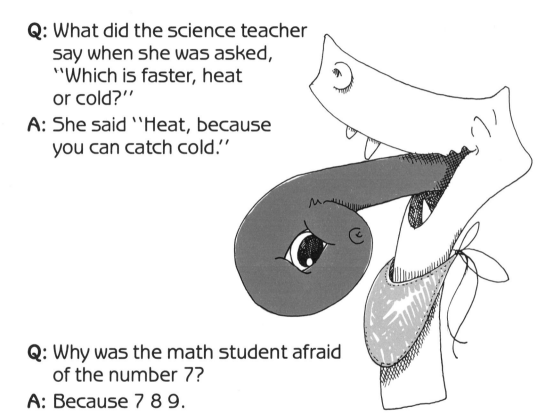

Q: Why was the math student afraid of the number 7?

A: Because 7 8 9.

Q: What did the vampire learn in school?
A: Puncturation.

Q: Why did the skeleton skip school?
A: It didn't have the guts for it.

Q: Why did Dracula go to school?
A: He was looking for the alphabat.

Q: Who haunts the school?
A: The school spirit.

Q: Where did the ghost go to learn?
A: High Ghoul.

Q: Who scared the students in the hall?

A: The Lockerness monster.

Q: What do you get when you cross a professor and a monster?

A: The Teacher from the Black Lagoon.

Q: Why did the teacher go to the beach?
A: He wanted to test the waters.

Q: What did the student have just before he got his report card?

A: Grade Expectations.

Q: Why did the report card sting?

A: It was all "B's."

Q: Why was it smooth sailing with the report card?

A: It was nothing but straight "C's."

Q: When is a report card like a sheep?

A: When the grades are B-A-A-B-A-A.

Q: Why couldn't the bookworm sneeze?

A: He had his nose in a book.

Q: What book is a good listener?

A: The school 'earbook.

Q: Why was the math book so sad?

A: It was full of problems.

Q: Why was the student afraid to go to school?

A: She didn't want to get stung by the spelling bee.

Q: How did the spelling bee champion correct the word "Beee?"

A: She used an "e"-raser.

Q: Why did the school add another floor of English classes?

A: They wanted another story.

Q: What did the school janitor say when they asked him about his job?

A: "It's picking up."

Q: Why did the fish go to school?

A: He heard they had bookworms.

Q: Why did the king go to school?

A: He heard they needed a ruler.

Q: Why did the dogs go to school?

A: They heard there was going to be a pup rally.

Q: Why did the classroom stink?

A: It was full of pew-pils.

Q: Why was the chess team in the dark?

A: They lost all their matches.

Q: What did the astronomy student get for taking second place?

A: The constellation prize.

Q: What was the teacher's favorite dessert?

A: Edu-cake.

Q: Why was the teacher unpopular?

A: He had no class.

Q: How boring was the teacher?

A: He even made the chalk bored.

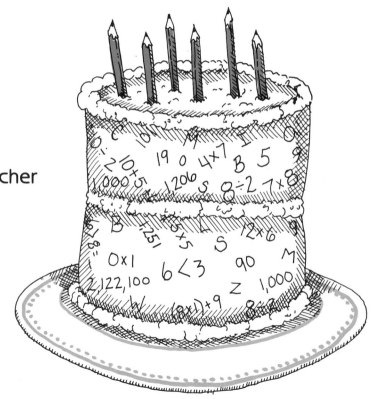

Q: Why was the failing student like Columbus?
A: He went down in history.

Q: Where did the student learn about morals?
A: In the principles office.

Q: Who in school is in charge of bad habits?
A: The vice-principal.

Q: Where do teachers send students who don't tell the truth?
A: To the lie-brary.

Q: How did the music teacher want his students to play?
A: Solo. Solo they couldn't be heard.

Q: Why was the best-liked teacher also the coolest?

A: Because she had lots of fans.

Q: Who was the best athlete in school?
A: Jim Class.

Q: How did the gym teacher travel?
A: She went coach.

Q: What do you need for music class?
A: A notebook.

Q: Why can't you whisper in school?
A: Because it isn't aloud.

Q: How happy was everybody when school finally ended?
A: Even the hands on the clocks applauded.

ABOUT THE AUTHOR

John Jansen and his wife, Michele, live in Minneapolis, Minnesota. John writes video scripts and screenplays and has written and performed stand-up comedy. He loves to tell bedtime stories that make his kids, Mick and Lauren, laugh. He really hopes that you get a laugh or two out of this book.

ABOUT THE ARTIST

Susan Slattery Burke loves to illustrate fun-loving characters, especially animals. To her, each of her characters has a personality all its own. She is most satisfied when the characters come to life for the reader as well. Susan lives in Minnetonka, Minnesota, with her husband, two daughters, and their dog and cat. Susan enjoys sculpting, reading, traveling, illustrating, and chasing her children around.

You Must Be Joking books

Alphabatty
Riddles from A to Z

Class Act
Riddles for School

Help Wanted
Riddles about Jobs

Here's to Ewe
Riddles about Sheep

Hide and Shriek
Riddles about Ghosts
and Goblins

Ho Ho Ho!
Riddles about
Santa Claus

Home on the Range
Ranch-Style Riddles

Hoop-La
Riddles about Basketball

I Toad You So
Riddles about Frogs and Toads

Off Base
Riddles about Baseball

On with the Show
Show Me Riddles

Out on a Limb
Riddles about Trees
and Plants

Out to Dry
Riddles about Deserts

Playing Possum
Riddles about Kangaroos,
Koalas, and Other Marsupials

Plugged In
Electric Riddles

Summit Up
Riddles about Mountains

Take a Hike
Riddles about Football

That's for Shore
Riddles from the Beach

Weather or Not
Riddles for Rain and Shine

What's Gnu?
Riddles from the Zoo

Wing It!
Riddles about Birds